Introduction

December can pass in a haze of busyness. There is so much to do to prepare for Christmas that, if we are not careful, we can arrive at 25 December with many jobs done only to discover that we are not ready to celebrate the birth of Jesus. This book isn't trying to give you more things to do, but to encourage you to take time to be ready for Christmas.

This booklet accompanies the popular **Love Life Live Advent children's booklet** (2014) and has the same actions for each day. In addition to a daily action it provides a short Bible reading, a reflection and a focus for prayer. Scattered through the booklet are also prayers and readings for each of the four Sundays of Advent. (Bear in mind that the First Sunday of Advent will occur before 1 December some years.)

As you prepare for Christmas, we hope that these readings, reflections and prayers will help you to go deeper and inspire you to make room for the manger.

1st Sunday of Advent

On the first Sunday of Advent we remember the Mothers and Fathers of the faith in the Old Testament; people like Abraham and Sarah, Moses and Miriam, David and Solomon (known as the patriarchs); people who first responded to God's call.

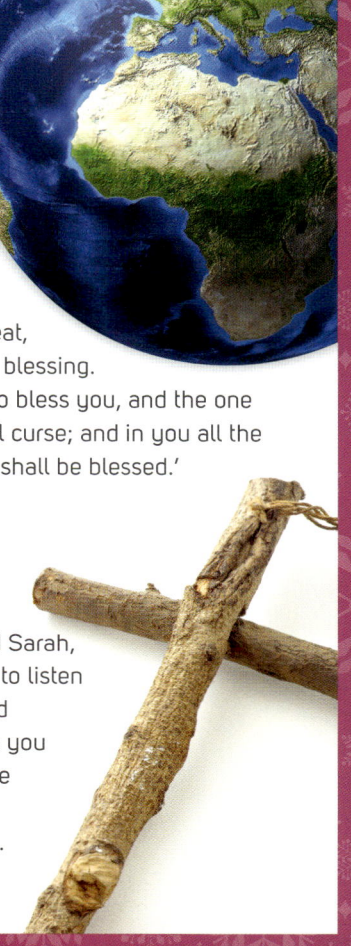

Read

Now the LORD said to Abram, 'Go from your country and your kindred and your father's house to the land that I will show you. I will make of you a great nation, and I will bless you, and make your name great, so that you will be a blessing. I will bless those who bless you, and the one who curses you I will curse; and in you all the families of the earth shall be blessed.'

Genesis 12.1–3

Pray

God of Abraham and Sarah, you gave them faith to listen when you spoke, and strength to go where you said. Help us to make room in our lives to hear your loving call. Amen.

1st Make room

> In the wilderness prepare the way of the LORD, make straight in the desert a highway for our God. **Isaiah 40.3**

Reflect

The importance of preparing yourself for God when he appears is a theme that runs throughout the Bible. Going into the wilderness was one way of preparing, since it removed distractions, allowing people to focus on God for whom they waited. Most of us can't go into the wilderness but we can make a space that helps us to focus on God.

Pray

that this Advent you will find the time and the space to encounter God.

Act

Make a place in your home where you will think about Advent, and make it special. Put your Advent calendar, candle and/or wreath there.

 **2nd Be generous**

> For you know the generous act of our Lord Jesus Christ, that though he was rich, yet for your sakes he became poor, so that by his poverty you might become rich. **2 Corinthians 8.9**

Reflect

Generosity is contagious. If someone is generous to you, it is so much easier to be generous in return. Generosity lies both at the heart of the Christian faith and of Christmas – we give to others because of Jesus Christ, who gave us everything he had so that we could experience the richness of his love.

Pray

that you might feel the love of Jesus and catch the contagious joy of generosity this Advent.

Act

Find a jar or pot to collect coins in. Collect them through Advent and then give them to a charity.

3rd Think deeply

I will give thanks to the LORD with my whole heart; I will tell of all your wonderful deeds. **Psalm 9.1**

Reflect

One of the most frequent commands in the Old Testament is to give thanks to God. Being thankful is transformative. It is all too easy to focus on those things that bring us misery and to overlook what brings us joy. Giving thanks teaches us to focus on the good things in our life; the more we do this the more aware of them we become.

Pray

Give thanks to God for the good things in your life.

Act

Think back over the last year: what made you most happy? Thank God for this.

4th Make room

> All who believed were together...
> they would sell their possessions and
> goods and distribute the proceeds to all,
> as any had need. **Acts 2.44–45**

Reflect

We live in a world in which some people have too
much; many others have too little. Even if we are not
rich, it can feel as though our homes are filled with
'stuff'. The early Christians tried to share everything
that they had. While most of us can't do this, we can
be inspired by their example and try to give away
what we no longer need.

Pray

that your life will
be more
filled with
love than
with things.

Act

Clear out a room,
a cupboard or a shelf
– give away as much
of it as you can.

5th Be thoughtful

> I give thanks to my God always for you because of the grace of God that has been given you in Christ Jesus. **1 Corinthians 1.4**

Reflect

People touch our lives in many ways, through actions as small as a smile on a grey and miserable day or as large as stepping in to save us when everything seems lost. Most of the time people touch our lives and go on their way having no knowledge of how they helped. Telling them might encourage them as much as they have encouraged you.

Pray

for someone who has been important to you this year.

Act

Take time to think of someone who has been important to you this year. Tell them in a Christmas card why they mean so much to you.

6th Slow down

> I praise you, for I am fearfully and wonderfully made. Wonderful are your works; that I know very well.
> **Psalm 139.14**

Reflect

Have you stopped recently to notice quite how wonderful the world is that God created? So often we rush through life at such a pace that we simply miss the beauty of birdsong, the many dappled colours of creation, the intricate detail of the created world.

Pray

Praise God for the wonder of the world he has created.

Act

Look carefully at a piece of holly or at a pine cone. Take time to notice its shape, its texture and its colours.

2nd Sunday of Advent

On the second Sunday of Advent we remember the prophets; people like Elijah, Isaiah and Micah. They listened to God's call and pointed others to what God had to say.

Read

A shoot shall come out from the stock of Jesse, and a branch shall grow out of his roots. The spirit of the Lord shall rest on him, the spirit of wisdom and understanding, the spirit of counsel and might, the spirit of knowledge and the fear of the Lord. His delight shall be in the fear of the Lord.

Isaiah 11.1–3a

Pray

God of Elijah, Isaiah and Micah, you gave them courage to speak your words of hope. Help us to make room in our lives for your love and peace to grow. Amen.

7th Be generous

> Those who are generous are blessed, for they share their bread with the poor.
> **Proverbs 22.9**

Reflect

For many of us this time of year can be a time of feasting and parties. Time and time again in the Bible God's people are called to remember those who are poor. In the midst of the plenty this year, take time to think of those who are hungry and are not sure where their next meal will come from.

Pray

for those in this country and across the world who will go to bed hungry tonight.

Act

Buy some food and give it to your local food bank.

8th Slow down

> If you then, who are evil, know how to give good gifts to your children, how much more will your Father in heaven give good things to those who ask him!
>
> **Matthew 7.11**

Reflect

God loves to give us good things. The created world testifies to the fact that God loves to pour out good things for us in wonderful, beautiful abundance. The problem is that we are often very bad at accepting these gifts. We rush on in our lives, so intent on the next task to be done that we miss what God yearns to give us.

Pray

Take time to feel God's love surrounding you.

Act

Take time out and do something really nice that you have wanted to do for a long time.

9th Be thoughtful

> Each of you must give as you have made up your mind, not reluctantly or under compulsion, for God loves a cheerful giver.
> **2 Corinthians 9.7**

Reflect

It is very easy for present-giving to become like a transaction – I give to you because you've given to me. True generosity, the kind that God models for us throughout the Bible, gives expecting nothing in return. This kind of generosity expresses love of the deepest kind and can, in an odd way, bring joy not just to the recipient but to the one giving as well.

Pray

for a generous and uncalculating heart.

Act

Think of someone you wouldn't usually buy a present for (and who may not buy you one), then give them something you think they would really like.

10th Be thoughtful

Consider the ravens: they neither sow nor reap, they have neither storehouse nor barn, and yet God feeds them. Of how much more value are you than the birds! **Luke 12.24**

Reflect

God does care for all the animals in his world but he calls us, as well, to be stewards of creation. It can be a chore in the cold and the wet to go out to top up a bird feeder or to express our care for God's world in another way, but in our caring we share with him in showing love for the world that he created.

Pray

for those who work in caring for the environment.

Act

Feed the birds. Maybe make a fat ball (see recipe on website).

 11th Be creative

> When I look at your heavens, the work of
> your fingers, the moon and the stars that
> you have established...
>
> **Psalm 8.3**

Reflect

God creates. The whole universe is the work of his
loving creativity. Human beings are made in the
image of God and as such are made to share in this
creativity. When we make or decorate something, we
join in with God's creative act, remembering his role
in creation and honouring it with our action.

Pray

Allow yourself to
wonder at the
intricacy of the
world God has
created and give
thanks for his care
for you.

Act

Make or buy
a Christmas
decoration and
give it to someone.

> Sing to the LORD, bless his name;
> tell of his salvation from day to day.
> **Psalm 96.2**

Reflect

We can become so used to Christmas carols that we sing them without noticing what they really say. Most Christmas carols are songs of praise to God for what he has done for us in sending his Son to be born in our world. Taking time to savour the words of a carol we know really well can bring it back to life again for us.

Pray

Give thanks to God for the gift of his Son.

Act

What is your favourite Christmas carol? Find the words to it, read them slowly and think about what it says (you can sing it too if you like!).

3rd Sunday of Advent

On the third Sunday of Advent
we remember John the Baptist
who told everyone
to prepare for Jesus.

Read

The beginning of the good news about Jesus Christ, God's Son, happened just as it was written about in the prophecy of Isaiah:

Look, I am sending my messenger before you. He will prepare your way, a voice shouting in the wilderness: 'Prepare the way for the LORD; make his paths straight.'

John the Baptist was in the wilderness calling for people to be baptized to show that they were changing their hearts and lives and wanted God to forgive their sins.

Mark 1.1–4 (CEB)

Pray

God of John the Baptist, you sent him to prepare people to welcome Jesus, your Son. Help us to make room in our lives that we might be ready to welcome him this Christmas. Amen.

13th Look forward

The flowers appear on the earth; the time of singing has come, and the voice of the turtle-dove is heard in our land.
Song of Solomon 2.12

Reflect

In the middle of winter it can feel sometimes as though the spring will never come. Spring brings with it a sense of new life and hope. While we cannot hurry the winter along, we can prepare ourselves for new life – a new life that comes at Christmas as well as in the spring months. As we look ahead during advent, we prepare ourselves inwardly for the life that comes from God.

Pray

that you will feel the joy of life in all its fullness deep within your heart.

Act

Plant some bulbs inside or outside, ready for the spring.

14th Think deeply

Here is my servant, whom I uphold, my chosen, in whom my soul delights; I have put my spirit upon him; he will bring forth justice to the nations.
Isaiah 42.1

Reflect

Many of us long for the world to be a better place; a place where all people can live in safety and peace. We are not alone in this. The prophet Isaiah reminds us that God yearned for the world to be like that too. His servant was to bring justice on earth so that it could be like heaven, full of justice and peace.

Pray

for justice and peace throughout the world.

Act

What do you wish for the world? Write a prayer saying what you hope for.
(You could write it on a nice piece of paper and hang it on the Christmas tree.)

15th Be creative

But Mary treasured all these words
and pondered them in her heart.
Luke 2.19

Reflect

The story of Christmas – a story that tells of God's great love for us, a love so great he sent his Son born as a baby to live among us – is almost too great a mystery to comprehend. Mary, Luke tells us, treasured everything that happened, everything that was said to her, so that she could ponder over them later. Advent invites us to take time to ponder, just like Mary did.

Pray

take time to ponder the mystery of God's love.

Act

Write a poem or draw a picture that says something about what Christmas means to you.

16th Be thoughtful

'Martha, Martha, you are worried and distracted by many things; there is need of only one thing.'
Luke 10.41–42

Reflect

Many of us live our lives at a hectic pace, a pace that increases as Christmas draws closer. Work, friends and family all crowd in, making demands on our time; demands we often welcome since they invite us to show love. In the gospel story Martha was distracted by showing love through hospitality but risked missing the opportunity to sit and listen to Jesus.

Pray

that in the midst of your busyness you will not miss Jesus this year.

Act

Think of someone who is very busy at this time of year. Offer to do something for them.

17th Slow down

For God alone my soul waits in silence,
for my hope is from him.
Psalm 62.5

Reflect

Our world, particularly in the run-up to Christmas, is a place of great activity and stimulation: lights twinkle, music plays, screens flicker, messages ping onto our phones and computers. This kind of stimulation is energizing and can be exciting but it can also distract us from the still small voice of God.

Pray

that this Advent you might know the peace that can come in stillness.

Act

Turn off the lights. Sit in darkness for a few minutes – what does it feel like?

18th Be creative

> I do not cease to give thanks for you as
> I remember you in my prayers.
> **Ephesians 1.16**

Reflect

We are often very good at thanking people for the things they have given us or for what they have done for us. The most important people in our lives, however, affect us not because of what they do or say but simply because of who they are. There is nothing they have to do; their very existence transforms our lives.

Pray

for those people who have touched and transformed your life by just being who they are.

Act

Make (or buy) some mince pies or Christmas biscuits and give them to someone to say thank you for who they are.

4th Sunday of Advent

On the fourth Sunday of
Advent we remember Mary,
the mother of Jesus,
who waited for his birth
just like we are waiting now.

Read

The angel said to her, 'Do not be afraid, Mary, for you have found favour with God. And now, you will conceive in your womb and bear a son, and you will name him Jesus. He will be great, and will be called the Son of the Most High, and the Lord God will give to him the throne of his ancestor David. He will reign over the house of Jacob for ever, and of his kingdom there will be no end.' **Luke 1.30–33**

Pray

God of Mary, you gave her the patience to wait with hope for your birth. Help us to make room in our lives for your joy as we wait for Christmas.
Amen.

19th Slow down

Jesus said to them, 'Come away to a deserted place all by yourselves and rest a while.' For many were coming and going, and they had no leisure even to eat.

Mark 6.31

Reflect

In the last few days before Christmas there can be lots of jobs to be done, as well as lots of people coming and going. This is part of the fun of the Christmas season and is something to be enjoyed. Allowing ourselves to slow down, rest a while and be with others in a leisurely way is restorative and lets us savour the good things.

Pray

the Lord's Prayer, but say it slowly with a pause between each phrase.

Act

Take time to watch one of your favourite Christmas films.

20th Think deeply

The light shines in the darkness, and the darkness did not overcome it.
John 1.5

Reflect

Candle flames suggest defiance in the face of darkness and despair. As they flicker in the darkness they appear to push it back, spreading light through the gloom. Jesus, the light of the world, came to push back the darkness of our world, to spread light, hope and joy in the midst of gloom, misery and futility.

Pray

that the light of God will shine brightly in our world, overcoming the darkness of hate and bitterness.

Act

Watch a candle flame. What colours can you see in it? What does it make you feel like?

21st Slow down

Out of the ground the LORD God made to grow every tree that is pleasant to the sight and good for food.
Genesis 2.9

Reflect

Genesis tells us that God made the world for human beings to enjoy. He didn't just grow any old trees but trees that are 'pleasant to the sight and good for food'. It seems a great shame, therefore, that we often speed through life without even noticing that they are there. God's gift of creation calls out to us to stop, to notice and to enjoy its beauty.

Pray

give thanks for the beauty and pleasure we can find in creation.

Act

Go for a walk. See what you notice. What colours can you see and what sounds can you hear?

22nd Slow down

> Bear with one another and, if anyone has a complaint against another, forgive each other; just as the Lord has forgiven you, so you must also forgive.
> **Colossians 3.13**

Reflect

As we approach the end of another year it is good to look back and reflect. When there are things to celebrate, it is right to remember and say thank you. When things have gone less well, when we have been hurt or have hurt others, then we need to say sorry, or to forgive and let go.

Pray

that God will give you the grace to let go of those things that have hurt you.

Act

Think back over the last year: what do you need to let go of before Christmas? Give it to God.

23rd Be thoughtful

> There was also a prophet, Anna the daughter of Phanuel, of the tribe of Asher. She was of a great age. **Luke 2.36**

Reflect

Years of watching and waiting had prepared the prophet Anna to recognize Jesus when his parents brought him to the Temple. Her wisdom was the kind that can only be gained through years of experience. During Advent we have been learning more of who Jesus is so that we might know him more fully when he comes.

Pray

that you may be ready to recognize and welcome Jesus as he comes to you.

Act

Find someone older than you and ask them what they remember about Christmas when they were a child.

24th Be thankful

O give thanks to the LORD, for he is good; for his steadfast love endures for ever. **1 Chronicles 16.34**

Reflect

When we get caught up in the hard work of getting things sorted for the big day, we can easily believe that everything depends on our own efforts. Taking a moment to pause and be thankful can remind us that all we have – even life itself – is a gift. Remembering the steadfast love of the giver might even take some pressure off us.

Pray

that you, and all whom you love, might feel peace this Christmas.

Act

As you make your final preparations for Christmas (getting out stockings, putting presents under the tree), take a moment to thank God for what he has already given you.

Christmas Day!

Today is Christmas day!
Celebrate the birth of Jesus.
See how many people
you can say
Happy Christmas to today!

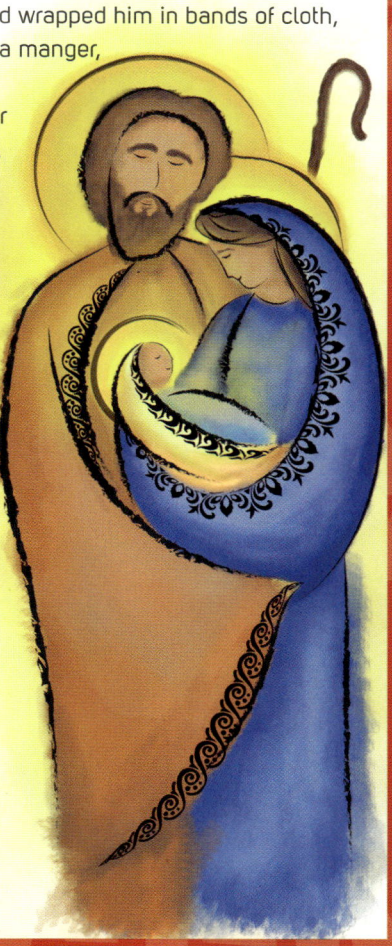

Read

While they were there, the time came for her to deliver her child. And she gave birth to her firstborn son and wrapped him in bands of cloth, and laid him in a manger, because there was no place for them in the inn.
Luke 2.6–7

Pray

God of all joy, You gave your Son to us at the first Christmas. Help us to make room for him in our lives today and every day. Amen.

FOR MORE ADVENT IDEAS AND SUPPORTING RESOURCES, PLEASE VISIT:

www.liveadvent.net

Published 2016 by Church House Publishing, Church House, Great Smith Street, London, SW1P 3AZ

Copyright © The Archbishops' Council 2012

Design by www.penguinboy.net

Email: copyright@churchofengland.org

Single ISBN 978 0 7151 4744 3
Pk 10 ISBN 978 0 7151 4745 0
Pk 25 ISBN 978 0 7151 4746 7

Scripture quotations are from the New Revised Standard Version of the Bible, Anglicized edition, copyright 1989 by the Division of Christian Education of the National Council of the Churches of Christ in the USA. Used by permission. All rights reserved.

Printed and bound in England by Core Publications